Pebble® Plus

Dogs, Dogs, Dogs

All about Rottweilers

by Erika L. Shores

Consulting Editor: Gail Saunders-Smith, PhD

CAPSTONE PRESS
a capstone imprint

Pebble Plus is published by Capstone Press,
1710 Roe Crest Drive, North Mankato, Minnesota 56003.
www.capstonepub.com

Library of Congress Cataloging-in-Publication Data
Shores, Erika L., 1976–
All about rottweilers / by Erika L. Shores.
p. cm.—(Pebble plus. dogs, dogs, dogs)
Includes bibliographical references and index.
Summary: "Full-color photographs and simple text provide a brief introduction to rottweilers"—Provided by publisher.
ISBN 978-1-4296-8728-7 (library binding)
ISBN 978-1-62065-296-1 (ebook PDF)
1. Rottweiler dog—Juvenile literature. I. Title.
SF429.R7S56 2013
636.73—dc23   2011049823

Editorial Credits
Veronica Correia, designer; Marcie Spence, media researcher; Kathy McColley, production specialist

Photo Credits
123RF: Bonzami Emmanuelle, 7, 21; Capstone Studio: Karon Dubke, 19; Dreamstime: Pixbilder, 3; iStockphoto:
JulianaLoomer, 17; Shutterstock: cynoclub, cover, 5, Degtyaryov Andrey Leonidovich, 1, 13, Tatiana Makotra, 9,
Waldemar Dabrowski, 11, Zuzule, 15

The author dedicates this book to Rob, Stephanie, Aria, and their guard dogs, Surly and Lily.

Note to Parents and Teachers

The Dogs, Dogs, Dogs series supports national science standards related to life science. This
book describes and illustrates rottweilers. The images support early readers in understanding
the text. The repetition of words and phrases helps early readers learn new words. This book
also introduces early readers to subject-specific vocabulary words, which are defined in the
Glossary section. Early readers may need assistance to read some words and to use the Table of
Contents, Glossary, Read More, Internet Sites, and Index sections of the book.

Printed in the United States of America in North Mankato, Minnesota.
052017   010554R

Table of Contents

Working Rotties

Rottweilers are named after Rottweil, a town in Germany. Long ago, these strong dogs herded livestock. Others pulled carts or worked as guard dogs.

Today, many rottweilers are

kept just as pets.

People often call them rotties.

Rotties are smart and loving.

The Rottweiler Look

Rotties are big dogs. They weigh up to 135 pounds (61 kilograms). Rotties grow as tall as 27 inches (69 centimeters) at the shoulder.

Rotties have large heads.
Their triangle-shaped ears hang
down against their heads.
Their dark brown eyes are
shaped like almonds.

Rotties have short, thick coats.

Their hair is black

with rust-colored markings.

Puppy Time

Ten to 12 rottweiler puppies are born in a litter. Rotties grow slowly. They are full-grown after about two years. Healthy rotties live up to 12 years.

Doggie Duties

Rotties need plenty of food and exercise every day. Because of their size, rotties eat more and need more exercise than smaller dogs do.

Rotties are born with a strong need to protect their owners. This instinct makes them dislike strangers. Responsible owners train rotties never to hurt anyone.

Loyal Rotties

Calm, loyal rotties often pick one family member to be closest to. A rottie might follow that person everywhere.

Glossary

coat—an animal's hair or fur

guard—to protect a place or person

herd—to bring together into a large group

instinct—a behavior that an animal is born with rather than learned

litter—a group of animals born at the same time to the same mother

livestock—animals raised for profit; cattle and sheep are livestock that were once herded by rottweilers

loyal—being true to something or someone

markings—patches of color on fur

responsible—having an important job or duty

rust—a red-brown color

Read More

Goldish, Meish. *Rottweiler: Super Courageous.* Big Dogs Rule. New York: Bearport Pub., 2012.

Green, Sara. *Rottweilers.* Dog Breeds. Minneapolis: Bellwether Media, 2011.

Johnson, J. Angelique. *Getting a Pet: Step-by-Step.* Step-by-Step Stories. Mankato, Minn.: Capstone Press, 2012.

Internet Sites

FactHound offers a safe, fun way to find Internet sites related to this book. All of the sites on FactHound have been researched by our staff.

Here's all you do:

Visit *www.facthound.com*

Type in this code: 9781429687287

 Check out projects, games and lots more at **www.capstonekids.com**

Index

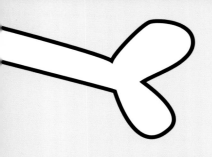

Word Count: 193
Grade: 1
Early-Intervention Level: 15